Make & Give Home
Apothecary

Stephanie Rose

LEISURE ARTS, INC. • Maumelle, Arkansas

LEISURE ARTS, INC. • Maumelle, Arkansas

Introduction

Self-care is somewhat of an afterthought these days. With hectic schedules and not enough downtime, people become exhausted, burnt out, and even worse, sick. It is critically important to our well-being to spend some time de-stressing and taking care of our bodies and minds. Yet many times it is left too far down the "To-Do" list. It often takes a caring friend or family member to remind us to slow down and look after ourselves in the way we would for others.

When we think about self-care, we often first think about what we put into our bodies, but frequently the products we put on our skin go overlooked. When I stopped to think about my own self-care, I researched the lotions, cosmetics, and perfumes I was using and realized I needed to make a change. I started experimenting with plant-based oils, waxes, and botanicals to replace the unrecognizable ingredients in store-bought skincare products.

Once I learned some basic recipes, I was hooked. From just a few ingredients—many of which I had in my kitchen or garden—I was able to make a wide variety of wholesome products. And I was astonished by how different I felt. The balms made my skin silky, the herbal baths eased away stiffness, and the fragrances lifted my mood. So I created a home apothecary filled with natural ingredients that could be made into a variety of lotions and potions.

Giving the gift of self-care is something you can do for those who deserve a little pampering. A soak in a warm tub filled with flower petals can soothe skin, while giving the mind a much-needed break. A massage from a loved

one can foster connection while easing aches and pains. The herbal therapy of botanicals can help with ailments from tired feet to lack of focus. By giving handcrafted herbal recipes from your home apothecary as gifts, you are sharing the sentiment of self-care as a priority.

Herbs, flowers, cocoa butter, plant oils, beeswax, and essential oils can make an abundance of homemade gifts that look good enough to be on the pages of a magazine. From decadent cocoa butter lip balm to botanical salt scrubs, luxurious bath bombs, stimulating massage bars, healing foot soaks, and more, the recipes contained in the following pages all draw on the healing power of plants in the most beautiful way possible.

And here is my gift to you: the projects in this book are so simple to make. You can easily replicate the techniques and personalize the recipes to suit your own tastes or those of the person you're giving them to. Once you've completed them, I've included a creative way to package each product for gift-giving that makes them extra special. Scale the projects up for wedding or event favors, give a single gift for a special occasion, or package a few of the projects together for a gift basket. No matter how you choose to give your gifts, be sure to make some extras for yourself. You certainly deserve some self-care too!

 For Rose and Leah
May your budding love of plants continue to blossom.

Contents

The Projects 14

Getting Started

Anyone can make gorgeous and healing bath and body products from natural, plant-based ingredients. These tried-and-true recipes are suitable for beginners, safe for children, and easy to scale up for large quantities (like wedding favors). The recipes are easy to follow and simple to customize. By changing up the botanicals, herbs, and essential oils, you can create a completely different product that uses the same base recipe.

There are two methods for making the projects in this book:

- **Measure and Mix:** Measure the ingredients, stir, and add the mixture to a container.

- **Melt and Pour:** Measure the ingredients, melt over heat and stir, then add to a container.

Both are easy! And the results are beautiful. The Measure and Mix method needs little explanation—you simply measure the ingredients and mix them together. The Melt and Pour method is also incredibly simple, but it has one extra step, melting the ingredients over heat. This method is used to make lip balms, massage bars, lotion bars, and bath melts.

Making Balms and Bars

Balms and bars come together by having the ingredients melted over moderate heat, stirred, and poured into a mold to harden. There are two ways of melting the ingredients together: the double boiler method and the microwave method.

THE DOUBLE BOILER METHOD

Double boilers come in many shapes and forms, but the general idea is to heat the contents of an inner pot in an outer pot filled with water. This will gently melt your ingredients and it is often quicker and heats the ingredients more evenly than the microwave method.

Measure the ingredients into the inner pot and fill the outer pot with a few inches of water. Use medium heat on most stovetops to keep the water in the outer pot warm, but not boiling. Stir the ingredients regularly while they melt and remove them from the heat as soon as the contents have liquefied. Overheating the ingredients can reduce their effectiveness and longevity. Once the ingredients are melted, add botanicals and essential oils, then pour into a mold to set.

THE MICROWAVE METHOD

The double boiler method is my preferred method for evenly and quickly melting ingredients. The recipes show double boiler configurations as examples. However, if you prefer to use the microwave, then follow these steps in place of the double boiler method listed in the recipe instructions.

Measure the ingredients into a heatproof measuring cup, mason jar, or other container that is safe to use in the microwave. Start heating the ingredients in 30-second intervals for large batches and 10-second intervals for smaller batches, then check and stir the ingredients at 10-second intervals until the solids have liquefied. It's important to keep the 10-second intervals because the ingredients can burn very quickly and ruin your project. Keep an eye on the microwave and it will be a handy tool for melting the ingredients for these projects. Once the ingredients are melted, add botanicals and essential oils, then pour into a mold to set.

Customization

The recipes that follow are proven to be marvelous blends, but if you want to switch them up, simply scale the recipe down and make a test batch with your substitutions. If you like the results, then go for it on a larger scale! If you don't, keep making adjustments until you find something you love.

Equipment

The recipes in this book are easy to make with standard equipment from your kitchen like a double boiler, a kitchen scale, mixing bowls, and canning jars. You don't need a lot of equipment to make these products at home, but here are a few of the essentials.

KITCHEN SCALE

A kitchen scale is an essential part of measuring the ingredients for each of these recipes. It can be tempting to try to convert the weight of the ingredients into baking measurements like cups and tablespoons, but I don't recommend doing this.

The ingredients come in many different forms and therefore might have a different weight per volume. For example, both beeswax and cocoa butter can come in solid blocks or in pastilles. A solid chunk of beeswax or cocoa butter will take up less volume but weigh more than the pastilles would in a measuring cup. To get the right mix for each of these recipes, use a kitchen scale and you'll be pleased with the results.

DOUBLE BOILER

For the Melt and Pour recipes, you will need either a double boiler or a microwave. I prefer a double boiler. You can use a traditional double boiler or make your own using a number of different things found in your kitchen, such as an electric pan filled with an inch or two of water and a heatproof container like a mason jar, measuring cup, or beaker.

You could also use a pot with a smaller pot or bowl set inside. The inner pot can be a small pot, recycled can, mason jar, Turkish coffee pot, metal or glass jug, or a metal or glass bowl. The water pot can be a large pot, pan, or even a baking pan. Set the inner pot on a small metal trivet inside the water pot to keep it raised off the bottom of the water pot and the heating element.

MOLDS

To make bars, bath bombs, and bath melts, you will need various molds. You can buy round molds specifically made for bath bombs or make smaller bath bombs in an ice cube tray. For melts and bars, silicone ice cube, candy, or soap molds work perfectly. There is such a wide variety available that you can certainly find a large selection of molds at a craft store or online.

Ingredients

Many of the ingredients required for the recipes in this book can be found right in your very own kitchen (or garden)! Some others will need to be specially purchased, but they are all easy to access online or in stores. All of the ingredients called for are organic, natural, and gentle on skin, but even so, it's best to test a small amount of any product beforehand to rule out allergies and sensitivities.

HERBS AND OTHER BOTANICALS

Many of the recipes call for fresh or dried herbs or flower petals. Harvesting plants from the wild or from the garden allows you to get in touch with nature and also harness the healing power of plants. You can always purchase dried botanicals if you can't find them fresh. Herbal tea is an excellent source for dried herbs. If you purchase herbs and botanicals, choose ones that are organic and culinary grade.

ESSENTIAL OILS

Essential oils are extracted from plants in a process that allows the purest essence of the fragrance and healing benefits to be captured in a tiny bottle. Many plants go into each bottle, so it's a very concentrated liquid, and you don't need to use a lot to make an impact in a recipe. When making Melt and Pour projects, the essential oils are added just before the ingredients are poured to ensure they don't become overheated and evaporate in the melting process.

Expiration Dates

Expiration dates for homemade products vary depending on a few factors. If the recipe is made of plant oil, cocoa butter, beeswax, and essential oils, the product will last as long as the expiration dates of those ingredients. Look at the labels on the ingredients and determine which has the soonest expiration date—this is the date your homemade product will expire.

When ingredients like herbs, botanicals, sugar, and water are added, they move up the expiration date. A sugar scrub should only be used for a few weeks before being discarded, as sugar is a breeding ground for bacteria and mold. Any products that have water added to them (for instance when they are used in the shower) will have a shortened shelf life. If you notice any signs of mold growth, odor, or discoloration, discontinue use immediately.

Vitamin E oil can be added to the recipes as a natural preservative to extend shelf life. If you don't plan to use a lot of Vitamin E, purchase it in capsules from a vitamin store and break open one or two capsules as needed to add to individual recipes.

PLANT OILS

Olive oil is very common and easy to find (you probably already have a bottle in your kitchen!), so it's an accessible choice to use as an ingredient for homemade skincare products. In your skincare products, there's no need to use virgin/extra virgin olive oil, so keep the fancier stuff for cooking and use a good, basic olive oil in your home apothecary. Olive oil is quite heavy and can clog pores, so it's best for products that will not be applied to the face. Olive oil hydrates and conditions skin well. It will add a bit of a yellow-green color to products and can have a strong scent—mix it with other ingredients so it doesn't become overpowering.

Grapeseed oil is a byproduct of winemaking made by pressing the natural oils out of grape seeds. The oil doesn't have much of an aroma and is very light, quick to absorb into skin, and full of antioxidants. Grapeseed oil is good for facial products and those with oily skin because it is so light and will hydrate skin without making it feel greasy.

Castor oil comes from the castor bean and has emollient properties. Unlike other oils, castor oil creates a solid film on the surface of skin, which works to lock in moisture and keep skin hydrated.

Sweet almond oil comes from pressing nuts from the sweet almond tree, so the oil contains the same beneficial nutrients and fatty acids you get from eating almonds. The oil is light, with a sweet fragrance, and works to maintain regular pH levels in skin, making it an effective ingredient for use on normal to dry skin types. It also contains Vitamin E, which protects and softens skin. Note that sweet almond oil is not safe for those who have nut allergies.

Coconut oil contains a high amount of fatty acids, has antibacterial and antimicrobial properties, and smells like a tropical vacation. It is especially effective at moisturizing the skin when combined with other ingredients. Coconut oil is good for hydrating sun-damaged skin and helps to prevent the look of aging. Unrefined, virgin/extra virgin coconut oil is best for use in homemade skincare products.

Cocoa butter comes from (you guessed it!) cocoa beans. It is an edible fat and is the main, essential ingredient in chocolate, which is why it smells so delicious. It is wonderful for hydrating skin and it contains antioxidants that you can absorb through your skin. Cocoa butter is a solid at room temperature, but heating it will transform it into a liquid that can be combined easily with other ingredients for a beauty recipe. Cocoa butter has a strong, chocolate aroma that holds well in recipes. If you don't care for the scent, it can be purchased in a processed form that has the scent removed. The recipes in this book use organic, raw cocoa butter that adds a mouth-watering aroma to the end products.

OTHER INGREDIENTS

Beeswax is used in a lot of beauty products because it works so well to bind various ingredients and create a more solid texture. It comes in pastilles and solid blocks. Pastilles are the most convenient form because you don't have to grate them as you do the solid beeswax, but they are also usually more expensive, so use the form that works best for you. When choosing beeswax for your home apothecary, make sure it is organic, cosmetic grade, and filtered. Unrefined, filtered beeswax has a heavenly honey scent that you will love.

Epsom salt is a mineral compound containing magnesium that can help relieve muscle pain. It has anti-inflammatory properties and works well as an exfoliator to remove dead, dry skin that can be itchy and uncomfortable.

How to Make Herb-Infused Oils

You can use any of the plant oils listed in the ingredients section exactly as they are in the recipes in this book, or you can make herb-infused versions and use them in the same way to add a little extra fragrance, color, and healing power.

To infuse oil with botanicals, the oil needs to be heated to allow the properties of the herbs to transfer to the oil. There are three different heating methods you can use: a stovetop, a slow cooker, or the sun.

Whatever heating method you choose, the basic steps are to pack a clean container full of dried herbs, pour oil over the herbs to submerge them, heat, and then strain the herbs out of the oil. It is important to use completely dried herbs as moisture can introduce bacteria and mold to the mixture.

My favorite oils to use for infusing are olive oil, sweet almond oil, and coconut oil. You can use any herbs that you like, but these are the ones I've found to work best:

HERB	BENEFITS
Lavender	Antibacterial properties, soothing scent, adds a purple-brown color to oil
Calendula	Very gentle, heals skin, adds a golden color to oil
Chamomile	Calming scent, antibacterial, helps clear up acne
Comfrey	Anti-inflammatory, pain relief
Sage	Anti-inflammatory, reduces redness and wrinkles
Mint	Energizing scent, pain relief, adds a dark color to oil
Rose	Increases skin's permeability, reduces discoloration and wrinkles

When your infused oil is ready, store it in a container with a tight-fitting lid and keep it in a cool, dark location. Generally, infused oil will last up to the expiration date on the original oil's package label. Olive oil should last for 2 to 3 years, and coconut oil will last for many years, although spoiling could happen more quickly if contaminants are introduced during the infusing process.

ON THE STOVETOP

Gently heat your herbs and oil in a double boiler on medium-low heat. If you are using coconut oil, heat it to liquefy it, then add the herbs. If you are using any other oil, first add your herbs to the double boiler, then pour the oil over top. Once the mixture is heated, turn the temperature to low and leave it for a few hours until it becomes very aromatic.

IN A SLOW COOKER

This method works well as long as you have a slow cooker with a very low heat setting. Add your ingredients to mason jars and place the jars inside the slow cooker. You do not need to add lids to the jars—just put the slow cooker lid on. Set the slow cooker to the lowest setting and leave it for 8 to 12 hours. If the temperature in the slow cooker becomes too warm, raise the oil jars up on a trivet or a washcloth to diffuse the direct heat.

IN THE SUN

Fill canning jars with herbs and pour oil over top until the herbs are submerged. Put the lids on the jars and set them outside in the sun for about 8 hours. Do this on a sunny day, but not at the peak of summer, as overheating the oils can remove some of their beneficial properties.

The Projects

Now that you have your home apothecary stocked with healing plants and gorgeous botanicals, it's time to create something wonderful. It's astonishing how just a few of these ingredients can transform into delicious-smelling balms, soothing bath treats, and gorgeous herbal gifts in the simplest of steps. The projects that follow show you a number of ideas and techniques that can give you a toolkit of skills to craft up a variety of homemade herbal gifts for everyone on your list. There is also plenty of room to play around with customizing your creations based on your personal tastes or the preferences of your loved ones. By keeping the basic ingredients the same, but switching out the fragrance and the botanicals used, you can make a completely different project. Change the mint essential oil to sweet orange in the Double Chocolate Mint Lip Balm and you have an equally tasty treat with a completely different personality. Swap rose petals for the coffee beans in the Coffee Massage Bar, and you will change the tone from invigorating to romantic. Use your creativity to play around and experiment. It's great fun to invent different blends, and even more fun to do the testing. I highly recommend that you try out each project and spend some time pampering yourself in the process.

Botanical Bath Salts

MAKES THREE 85-GRAM TEST TUBES

There's nothing more healing than time spent soaking in a warm tub. Using botanicals, essential oils, and bath salts is a luxurious way to pamper your skin and detoxify your body. A trio of botanical bath salts allows you to give the gift of three unique healing baths for different moods. Lavender bath salts are wonderful before bedtime and allow your body to relax into a deep sleep. Rose bath salts are soothing and help to repair skin, plus rose is the flower of romance. Citrus bath salts can help cheer you up when you've got the blues.

INGREDIENTS

- 270 grams Epsom salt

RECIPE #1
- ¼ cup dried lavender buds
- 10 drops lavender essential oil

RECIPE #2
- ¼ cup dried rose petals
- 10 drops essential oil blend that includes rose

RECIPE #3
- ¼ cup dried citrus rind and zest
- 10 drops citrus essential oil blend or any combination of sweet orange, grapefruit, lime, lemon, tangerine, and bergamot

MATERIALS

- Three 85-gram glass test tubes with lids or corks

EQUIPMENT

- Kitchen scale
- Funnel or scrap paper

Lovely Lavender

Lavender has been added to baths since Roman times because of its antibacterial properties and pleasing scent. The fragrance of lavender is used in aromatherapy to calm and relax and is purported to aid insomnia, so choose lavender bath salts for a before-bedtime soak and settle in for a restful slumber.

MAKE IT! • BOTANICAL BATH SALTS

1 Gather all of your ingredients and set them out in your work area.

2 Using a funnel (or a sheet of scrap paper rolled into a funnel), fill each test tube with Epsom salt, leaving one inch of space at the top.

3 Pour the Epsom salt out of one of the test tubes into a small mixing bowl. Add the dried botanicals for Recipe #1 and mix to combine.

4 Use a dropper to add the essential oil for Recipe #1. Mix well and refill the test tube.

5 Repeat Steps 3 through 4 with the ingredients for Recipe #2 and Recipe #3.

6 When you have filled all three of the test tubes with a different fragrance and botanical blend, top them with the corks or lids that they came with.

Package this trio of botanical bath salts in a set of glass test tubes, each topped with a cork. Wrap decorative wire around each test tube and toss in a dried bay leaf. Pop them into a burlap drawstring bag to give them as a set.

Tub Tea

MAKES FOUR ½-CUP TUB TEA BAGS

Herbs are wonderful in the bath, but floating botanicals are not for everyone. Some people love to bathe in a sea of flower petals, while others may care for a more pristine bath. A tub tea allows you to give someone the full herbal bath experience without the botanicals to clean up after the water has drained. Using paper tea filters means that these tub teas can be tossed right in the compost bin after the bath.

INGREDIENTS

- 8 drops essential oil of your choice (optional)
- 1 cup Epsom salt
- 1 cup blend (see at right)

MATERIALS

- 4 large paper tea filters

EQUIPMENT

- Sewing machine

BLEND INGREDIENTS

While the other recipes in this book are measured by weight, this recipe is measured by volume. Each tea filter will hold half a cup of ingredients, half of which will be Epsom salt and half of which will be dried botanicals, herbs, salts, and other ingredients. Create a 1-cup blend using any of these ingredients that you would like to include.

- Ground oatmeal
- Powdered milk or goat's milk
- Baking soda
- Salts like Himalayan pink salt or dead sea salts
- Dried flowers like calendula, rose, or lavender
- Dried herbs like mint, ginger, or chamomile
- Dried spices like star anise or turmeric
- Dried herbal or green tea leaves

Cleanse and Cure with Oatmeal

Oatmeal soothes skin and won't strip away the skin's natural oils, making it ideal for those with dry or sensitive skin. Oatmeal is a natural anti-inflammatory that can reduce pain and itching caused by sunburn, dry skin, and rashes.

1 Select the ingredients you want to include in your tub tea and make a 1-cup blend.

2 Mix the Epsom salt and blend of your chosen ingredients in a bowl or jar. If desired, add the essential oil of your choice and stir to combine.

3 Fill each tea bag with a few heaping spoonfuls of the mixture (about ½ cup).

4 Seal the tea bags by folding the top over a few times, and then use a sewing machine and a decorative stitch to sew the bags shut.

***Tip* |** The paper tea bags can be tossed in your compost bin after the bath so there is no messy cleanup. You could also package them in a cotton muslin drawstring bag for a reusable tub tea, but the remaining ingredients will need to be discarded and replaced after each bath.

Use a letter stamp set and a gold pen to create a tag with the instructions, "Add one bag to a warm bath. Enjoy." Attach the tags with mini wooden clothespins and your tub teas are ready to gift!

Herbal Foot Soak

MAKES 2 CUPS OF FOOT SOAK

Our feet work so hard for us—taking us on adventures, being squeezed into gorgeous shoes, and keeping us grounded. And yet they often don't get the care they deserve. Soaking them in warm water with salts and botanicals is a quick and easy way to pamper your hardworking feet and give your whole body a bit of rest and relaxation. A foot soak can relieve muscle aches and stiffness, reduce inflammation, and improve circulation. It can also soften dry skin and deodorize your feet. But, more than anything else, it feels fantastic!

INGREDIENTS

- 2 cups Epsom salt
- 8 drops pure lavender essential oil
- 6 drops mint essential oil
- 2 drops eucalyptus essential oil
- 2 drops rosemary essential oil
- 1 teaspoon dried comfrey root powder
- ½ cup dried mixed flower petals, lavender buds, and mint leaves

MATERIALS

- Decorative glass jar
- Wooden scoop

Relieve Foot Pain

Since ancient Roman times (at the very least), comfrey root has been used to treat bruises, aches, and pains. It contains rosmarinic acid, an anti-inflammatory that can be a powerful tool for pain relief. Comfrey root also has a high content of allantoin, which stimulates new skin cell growth and soothes dry, itchy skin. Perfect for soothing tired, achy feet at the end of a long day!

1 Prepare your ingredients. Choose an attractive combination of botanicals to add color to the blend. They will steep in the warm water to add an herbal infusion. The bulk of the healing benefits come from the Epsom salt, comfrey root powder, and essential oils, so the mix of botanicals is up to you.

2 Fill a bowl with Epsom salt.

3 Add the essential oils and stir to combine.

Get Fresh

Sometimes feet start to smell like, well, feet. Eucalyptus, mint, lavender, and rosemary have natural deodorizing and antibacterial properties that can make feet feel and smell fresh again, even after a day trapped inside soggy boots or sweaty sneakers.

4 Add the comfrey root powder and dried mixed botanicals.

5 Scoop the mixture into a decorative glass jar.

6 Add a wood scoop to the jar with the mixture before closing the lid.

Creating a clay gift tag is easy to do with air-dry clay. Roll out a 3" circle of terracotta air-dry clay until it is ¼" thick. Press a stem of flowers into the center of the clay, then roll over it gently with the rolling pin. Remove the flowers and use a heart-shaped cookie cutter to cut out a heart with the flower imprint in the center. Use a skewer to make a hole at the top of the heart for twine. When the clay is dry, lightly brush the front with white craft paint. Tie jute twine around the jar a few times and attach the clay heart.

Floral Bath Bombs

MAKES FOUR 2½"-ROUND BATH BOMBS

These homemade fizzing bath bombs will turn your bathtub into a hot tub. When skin softening baking soda is combined with citric acid and added to the bath water, the effervescence disperses essential oils and botanicals into the water for an aromatherapy spa experience. Adding a few dried violets into the mold makes for an extra special treat. Other dried flowers that would work well for a bath bomb are rose petals, calendula, chamomile, lavender, and bachelor's buttons.

There are many bath bomb recipes out there, but this one is the most consistently successful for me. I've found it's less about the ingredients and more about the technique. Follow the instructions carefully and you should have a set of gorgeous bath bombs on your hands.

INGREDIENTS

- 250 grams non-aluminum baking soda
- 125 grams citric acid
- 125 grams organic cornstarch
- 125 grams Epsom salt
- 100% pure witch hazel
- 20 drops grapefruit essential oil or a floral blend like rose, geranium, or lavender
- ¼ cup dried calendula petals
- Pressed, dried violets

EQUIPMENT

- Kitchen scale
- Small spray bottle
- Round, two-piece bath bomb mold

Natural Colorants

If you would like to add color to your bath bombs, use natural colorants and add them in small amounts before you add the witch hazel. Start with just a pinch of color and add more gradually as needed to get a deeper color. Keep in mind that any colorant will leave a residue on the bathtub, which means clean-up will be needed after the bath. These ground-up dried herbs and other organics work well as natural colors in bath bombs.

- **Green:** spirulina, sage powder
- **Golden yellow:** safflower powder
- **Yellow:** turmeric
- **Yellow-Orange:** annatto seed powder

- **Red-Orange:** paprika
- **Pink:** madder root
- **Purple:** Ratan Jot
- **Brown:** cocoa powder

1 Prepare the mold before you start working on your bath bomb so it is ready to use right away in Step 5. Add a few flowers to the center of one half of the mold, facing them toward the mold and away from you.

2 In a large bowl, add the baking soda, citric acid, cornstarch, and Epsom salt and mix well. Add the essential oil and mix again.

3 Using a small spray bottle filled with witch hazel, spray the surface of the mixture 6–8 times. Working quickly, blend the witch hazel into the mixture using your hands. Continue adding a few spritzes of witch hazel at a time and blending it rapidly until the mixture has the consistency of damp sand. It should feel dry but hold its shape when formed into a ball with your hands.

4 Add the calendula petals and mix them in with your hands.

5 Spray the flowers you added to the mold with witch hazel, just a tiny spritz to help them adhere to the bath bomb.

6 Working quickly, add the mixture to each half of the mold, firmly pressing it into the mold with your thumbs. Keep topping off the mix until you have no give at all when pressing it into the mold. You really want to pack the mixture in there tightly.

7 To finish, over-fill each half of the mold and press them together firmly. Clean off any excess mixture that escapes from between the two mold halves.

Place the bath bomb in a wooden box with the flower facing up so you can see that pretty detail. Line the box with shredded paper printed with a message like, "You are the bomb." To make the shredded message paper, repeat the sentence multiple times in a document using an 11-point font with 10-point spacing after each paragraph and 1.15 line spacing. Print on decorative paper and either put it through a paper shredder, lining up the blades to be between the paragraphs, or cut the strips by hand. Crinkle the strips by folding them like an accordion, then use them to create a padded nest for the bath bomb.

8 Gently tap the outside of the mold to release the bath bomb. Carefully lay the bath bomb on a tray and let it dry undisturbed for 24 hours. Repeat Steps 5–8 with the remaining mixture.

Troubleshooting

If your bath bomb crumbles, the mixture was too dry. If the mixture expands and fizzes, it is too wet. If the bath bomb sticks to the mold or cracks as it dries, the mixture may be too wet. The trick to mastering bath bombs is to get the mixture to the right consistency. Once you have the technique, then making bath bombs is easy.

Lavender and Cocoa Butter Bath Melts

MAKES 12 SMALL BATH MELTS

Warning: the mouthwatering scent of these luxurious bath melts may make you want to eat them. Don't get me wrong, the ingredients are so natural and wholesome that you absolutely could eat them, but you'll enjoy them much more in the bath. The calming fragrance of lavender will relax your mind, while the cocoa butter and coconut oil will melt and absorb into your skin, leaving it soft, smooth, and deeply hydrated. Just pop them into the hot water and soak for at least 20 minutes. These melts are a simple way to make any bath feel like a mini spa retreat—perfect for those days when you need a little extra self-care without any extra effort!

INGREDIENTS

- 55 grams cocoa butter
- 25 grams coconut oil
- 20 drops lavender essential oil
- 1 teaspoon dried lavender flowers

EQUIPMENT

- Kitchen scale
- Double boiler
- Silicone ice cube tray for mold

Treat Yourself with Cocoa Butter

Unrefined cocoa butter smells like a light, honeyed version of chocolate. It has intense hydrating properties and, when mixed with coconut oil, will seal moisture into the skin, leaving your whole body feeling and smelling wonderful.

add 1-2 melts per bath

1 Prepare and weigh the ingredients.

2 Melt the cocoa butter and coconut oil in a double boiler. Stir constantly and keep a watchful eye on them. You want them to just reach the melting point and not overheat.

3 When the cocoa butter and coconut oil have melted and combined, add the essential oil and stir well. Immediately pour into a silicone mold.

4 Sprinkle the dried lavender buds on top of the hot oil, dividing them evenly between the bath melts.

5 Move the silicone mold to the refrigerator to cool for 2 hours until set. Store the finished bath melts in the fridge or a cool place if your house is warm.

After Bath Clean-Up

These bath melts are small, and much of the oil will absorb into your skin, but even so, some oil residue will remain on the sides of your tub. To clean up easily, use a kitchen scrubber with a handle that can be filled with soap. Fill the reservoir with biodegradable dish soap and give the sides of the tub a quick wash. Rinse with water and you are ready for your next bath.

Package a handful of these bath melts in a box lined with shredded parchment paper. Add a label on the outside of the box that reads, "Lavender Bath Melts" and a label on the inside that reads, "Add 1-2 melts per bath."

Coffee Bean Massage Bars

MAKES FOUR 50-GRAM BARS

Solid massage bars are a great way to soften skin without the mess of massage oil. The beeswax, cocoa butter, and coffee beans add so much fragrance to this recipe that no additional essential oils are needed for aroma. The soothing scent combination, skin-nourishing ingredients, and relaxation of a massage all come together for an at-home spa experience that will make weary muscles and minds feel renewed.

INGREDIENTS

- 65 grams beeswax
- 65 grams grapeseed oil
- 90 grams cocoa butter
- 2 tablespoons roasted coffee beans

EQUIPMENT

- Kitchen scale
- Double boiler
- Oval silicone soap mold

Wake Up Tired Skin with Coffee

The coffee beans in these massage bars serve a dual purpose. First, those little round beans are the perfect shape to add a texture in the massage bar that feels great on your skin. Second, coffee antioxidants help calm inflamed skin. This makes for a massage bar that's both stimulating and calming at the same time. This might be the perfect gift for someone you hope will give YOU a massage!

MAKE IT! • COFFEE BEAN MASSAGE BARS

1 Weigh the beeswax, grapeseed oil, and cocoa butter and add them to the top pot of a double boiler.

2 Divide the roasted coffee beans evenly between four of the cups in the silicone soap mold.

3 Heat the ingredients in the double boiler, stirring until they have all melted together.

4 Pour the ingredients into the silicone mold, dividing the contents equally.

5 Leave the massage bars undisturbed until they are set. If you are making them in a warm room, move the silicone tray into the fridge to help them firm up.

6 Remove the bars from the mold and store them in the refrigerator when not in use.

Package a single massage bar in a burlap drawstring bag (which looks like a miniature burlap coffee sack!). Use letter stamps to create a label with the name of the bar. Give the edges of the label a burnished look by brushing them across an ink pad. A small grapevine heart attached to the tag and jute twine finishes off the wrapping.

Calendula Lotion Bars

MAKES EIGHT 57½-GRAM BARS

Calendula is more than just a garden beauty—it also has a long-standing reputation as a natural anti-inflammatory skincare treatment. These lotion bars are made with grapeseed oil infused with calendula petals to give them a beautiful golden hue and all the delightful skin properties of calendula. These lotion bars glide on your skin easily, are absorbed quickly, and don't leave you with a greasy feeling.

INGREDIENTS

- 200 grams calendula-infused grapeseed oil
- 100 grams virgin coconut oil
- 100 grams beeswax
- 60 grams cocoa butter
- A pinch of dried calendula petals (optional)
- 40 drops lavender essential oil (optional)

EQUIPMENT

- Kitchen scale
- Double boiler
- Silicone flower soap mold

The Healing Herb

Throughout history, calendula has been in ointments, salves, and poultices to treat burns, wounds, bruises, and inflammation of all kinds. Calendula speeds up the growth of tissue, which means it does wonders for healing minor cuts and scrapes quickly. It is also moisturizing and extremely gentle, so it is a good choice for children or those with sensitive skin.

1 Infuse the grapeseed oil with calendula petals as described on pages 12–13.

2 Weigh the grapeseed oil, coconut oil, beeswax, and cocoa butter and add them to the top pot of a double boiler.

3 Heat the ingredients in the double boiler, stirring until they have all melted together.

4 If you're adding the lavender essential oil, stir it in now. Pour the ingredients into the silicone mold, dividing the contents equally. Sprinkle with calendula petals while still hot (optional).

5 Leave the lotion bars undisturbed until they are set. If you are making them in a warm room, move the silicone mold into the fridge to help them firm up.

6 Remove the bars from the mold and store them in the refrigerator when not in use.

Package up one lotion bar in a metal tin on a bed of shredded paper and calendula petals. Create a 2½"-diameter canning lid label and print it on craft paper. Use a 2½" hole punch to cut out the label as a perfectly round circle. Add the label to the top of the tin and the lotion bar is ready to gift.

Double Chocolate Mint Lip Balm

MAKES SIX 4½-MILLILITER TUBES

If you like chocolate as a dessert, you will love it in your lip balm! This lip balm has both cocoa butter and cocoa powder in it, giving it double the chocolaty skin benefits. Cocoa butter is ultra moisturizing and it is readily absorbed into the skin because it melts at body temperature. Cocoa powder is rich in skin anti-oxidants and gives the lip balm a hint of color. The mint essential oil adds a cooling tingle to this luxurious lip balm and pairs perfectly with the chocolate.

INGREDIENTS

- 8 grams coconut oil
- 8 grams grapeseed oil
- 6 grams castor oil
- 6 grams beeswax
- 4 grams cocoa butter
- ½ teaspoon organic cocoa powder
- 10 drops peppermint essential oil

MATERIALS

- Six 4½-milliliter clear lip balm tubes

EQUIPMENT

- Kitchen scale
- Small double boiler with an inner pot that has a pour spout and handle

Mint Conditioning

In addition to adding a flavorful zing to the already delicious chocolate scent of this lip balm, mint essential oil tingles, cools, and invigorates lips while infusing them with vitamins that help to condition, repair, and protect dry, chapped skin.

1 Measure the coconut, grapeseed, and castor oil, along with the beeswax and cocoa butter, into a small double boiler. The top pot should be something with a handle and a pour spout so that it is easy to fill the lip balm tubes from the pot.

2 Put the double boiler on medium heat and stir the ingredients regularly until they are all melted together.

3 Take the pot off the heat and add the cocoa powder. Stir well with a small whisk. Add in the essential oil. Stir well with a small whisk.

4 Twist each lip balm tube to be sure the risers are all set to the bottom. Carefully pour the lip balm into the tubes, filling each tube so the center screw is just covered. You should have some mixture leftover.

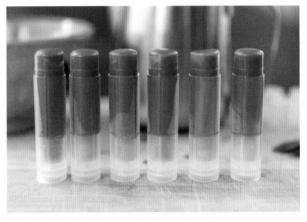

5 Let the lip balm cool in the tubes, then warm up the remaining mixture in the pot and use it to top off each tube. Filling the tubes in two steps like this ensures you won't have a depressed top or a hole in the center of your lip balm. If this happens, add a little bit more mixture to the top of the depressed area and pass a flame over the top of the lip balm to melt the top so it is smooth.

Create lip balm tube labels on the computer and print them on a sheet of colored craft label paper. The label size should be 1.69" x 2.125". When creating your designs, leave extra space at the top and bottom of each label, as they will overlap when wrapped around the tubes. Some lip balm tubes have a line down the side to help you line up the labels.

Honey Dandelion Lip Scrub

MAKES ONE 30-GRAM POT

Sure, you're familiar with dandelions, but have you ever smelled one? Their fragrance can range from an earthy smell to something quite sweet, but when the blossoms are picked at the right time, they have the aroma of honey. This isn't surprising because they are one of the first food sources for bees each year. The flowers also make wonderful infused oil that is great for chapped lips. Paired with honey and sugar, this scrub makes lips very kissable.

INGREDIENTS

- 20 grams sugar
- 5 grams dandelion-infused olive oil
- 2 grams honey

MATERIALS

- Small glass pot

EQUIPMENT

- Kitchen scale

> ### Healing Honey
> Honey has natural anti-bacterial properties and a ton of antioxidants that nourish and repair skin. It moisturizes, soothes, and stimulates tissue regeneration, making it a wonderful ingredient to relieve chapped, irritated lips.

1 Infuse olive oil with dandelion flowers following the instructions on pages 12–13.

2 Lay out your ingredients.

3 Set a small dish on the kitchen scale and set it to zero. Add the sugar.

4 Zero the scale and add the honey and oil. Mix them together well. If you like the consistency, you can package it up now. If you would like it to be wetter, add more oil. If you would like it to be drier, add more sugar.

5 Spoon the mixture into a small, glass pot. To use, apply a pea-sized amount to your lips and massage it in until the sugar has dissolved. Rinse with cool water and a cloth. Apply the lip balm of your choice. Store in a small, airtight container in the fridge for up to 30 days.

Foraging for Botanicals

The best botanicals are homegrown or purchased from reputable sources that have not sprayed or treated them with any pesticides or herbicides. People are notorious for dousing dandelions in chemicals to remove them from their pristine lawns, so when foraging, look for dandelions in meadows or yards that you know have not been treated with chemical pesticides and herbicides. Those are not the ingredients you want to add to your skin!

honey
dandelion
lip
scrub

Create a label on craft label paper and make a small tag with a bee stamp. Burnish the edges of the label and the tag by dragging them across a black ink pad. Attach the label to the top of the jar and attach the tag to the string of a small cotton muslin drawstring bag. Put the jar in the bag to deliver the lip scrub to your recipient.

Peppermint Coconut Sugar Scrub

MAKES 400 GRAMS OF SUGAR SCRUB

Peppermint and coconut pair perfectly when it comes to brightening up your skin and your day. Mint has a cooling effect on the skin and coconut oil is a powerful skin moisturizer. Plus, the fresh and tropical aroma will do wonders for your mood. This is a scrub that will make your skin smooth and soft, without the need to apply lotion after the shower.

INGREDIENTS

- 250 grams sugar

- 125 grams virgin coconut oil, softened

- 1 mint tea bag

- 10 drops peppermint essential oil

- Spirulina powder (optional)

MATERIALS

- Jar with lid

EQUIPMENT

- Kitchen scale

Deep Sea Greens

Spirulina is freshwater algae that heals skin and draws out toxins. Its deep green color adds a lot of personality to your home apothecary creations. Spirulina is also a popular superfood that is often added to green smoothies and supplements. Purchase it at a natural food store or a vitamin store in capsules and use one or two when you want to color a recipe.

1 Lay out your ingredients. Set the coconut oil out in a warm place so that it softens but does not completely melt. Look for the consistency of softened butter as called for when baking.

2 In a bowl, cream together the sugar and the coconut oil.

3 Empty the contents of a tea bag into a small bowl. Sprinkle the herbs into the sugar scrub. You can add as much or as little as you would like, keeping in mind that adding more herbs can make the scrub more abrasive.

4 To give the scrub a minty green color, add in some spirulina powder as a natural colorant (optional).

5 Add the peppermint essential oil.

6 Stir the ingredients together and scoop into a lidded jar.

Tea Time!

The availability of herbal teas means there is an endless supply of dried herbs available to stock your home apothecary. Simply break open a bag of organic herbal or green tea and use the dried herbs inside as an addition to your favorite plant-based beauty recipes.

Package the scrub in a jar with a chalkboard label, then use a liquid chalk pen to write the name of the scrub. Wrap jute twine around the top of the jar, just under the lid, and tie in a bow.

Healing Himalayan Pink Salt Scrub

MAKES ONE 250-GRAM JAR OF SCRUB

Don't let the pretty pink color of this scrub fool you into thinking it's all shine with no substance. The salt exfoliates and smoothes skin, while nourishing minerals penetrate skin to heal, detoxify, and rejuvenate. The rose petals and fragrant essential oil make this recipe healing and calming for both body and mind. All that and pink too? What's not to love?

INGREDIENTS

- 200 grams pink Himalayan sea salt

- 50 grams coconut oil

- 25 grams rose-infused sweet almond oil

- 8 drops rose geranium essential oil

- Dried rose petals (optional)

MATERIALS

- Small, airtight container

EQUIPMENT

- Kitchen scale

In the Pink

The pretty pink color of Himalayan salt is more than just pleasing to the eye—it is caused by iron and other minerals in the salt. The beneficial minerals are easily absorbed through the skin and help to heal damaged muscle tissue. The minerals also work to draw out impurities and detoxify while you soak, so you just might come out of the bath feeling like a new person.

1 Infuse sweet almond oil with rose petals following the instructions on pages 12–13.

2 Lay out your ingredients. Set the coconut oil out in a warm place so that it softens but does not completely melt. Look for the consistency of softened butter as called for when baking.

3 Weigh the sea salt and coconut oil on a kitchen scale.

4 Mix the sea salt, infused almond oil, and coconut oil together well. If you like the consistency you can package it up now. If you would like it to be wetter, then add more oil. If you would like it to be drier, add more salt. Add the essential oil and stir to combine.

5 Top with dried rose petals (optional) and store in a small, airtight container in the fridge for up to 30 days.

This Himalayan pink salt scrub is best when applied before a warm bath. Massage into wet skin all over the body and soak in a warm bath for at least 20 minutes. Rest, relax, and dry your skin thoroughly after the bath. Bring a cool glass of water to the bath with you as detoxification can be powerful.

You may feel a bit woozy right afterward. Drink at least two 8-ounce glasses of water during and within an hour after the bath. If this routine is being done before bed, you should have a wonderful night's rest. In the day, give yourself an extra 30 minutes to relax after the bath, then jump up and get on with your day.

Add dried rose petals to the top of the scrub before adding a piece of lace and securing it with the lid. Tie a ribbon around the edge of the lid. A handwritten or printed label finishes off the look.

Aromatherapy Perfume

MAKES ONE 10-MILLILITER AROMATHERAPY PERFUME

Roller bottles are popular in aromatherapy as a way to apply an individual dose of herbal benefits for a variety of different moods and ailments. Roller bottles can also make beautiful perfume bottles. By replacing lab-created fragrances with naturally occurring essential oils, you'll not only smell good, you'll feel pretty good too.

Blending essential oils is a skill that takes practice. To get started, take a few of the scents you are usually drawn to and hold the open bottles to your nose. When you breathe in the combination of fragrances, you'll learn what you like and what you don't.

When you find a combination you like, spend some time blending the oils together using different ratios to come up with a fragrance that works for you. For the strongest-scented oils, start with only one drop and add more if it's not strong enough. There are some scents—like lemongrass and cinnamon—that are so strong they can take over the entire blend.

INGREDIENTS

- 9 milliliters carrier oil of your choice

- 10 drops essential oil blend

- Fresh and dried flowers and herbs

MATERIALS

- One 10-milliliter glass roll-on bottle

Understanding Notes

The fragrance characteristics of essential oils are classified as "notes." Specifically top notes, middle notes, and base notes. Top notes are light, fresh, fast-acting, and tend to evaporate very quickly. This is usually the first scent you smell in a blend. Middle notes help to balance the blend. You might not smell the middle note right away, but the soft fragrance may become apparent after a few minutes. Base notes are very strong and heavy, grounding the blend with their long-lasting diffusion. Balance your perfume creations by blending different notes together to make the end result complex and alluring. Here are some examples.

- **Top notes:** bergamot, lemongrass, grapefruit, orange, geranium, peppermint, eucalyptus

- **Middle notes:** lavender, rose, mandarin orange, cypress, cinnamon bark

- **Base notes:** patchouli, cedarwood, sandalwood, frankincense, ginger

1 Spend some time blending essential oils to come up with a fragrance that works for you. Collect fresh or dried petals and leaves to use in the bottle. Prepare the roller bottle by removing the lid and roller ball.

2 Fill the bottle with the carrier oil. Choose fractionated coconut oil if you don't want your perfume to have any color. The other oils will be in various shades of amber and green (grapeseed oil is shown here).

3 Add 10 drops of your essential oil blend to the bottle.

4 Add a combination of fresh and dried flowers, leaves, or petals into the oil to decorate the bottle.

5 Pop the roller ball lid onto the glass vial. Shake well to combine the oils.

6 Leave the blend for 24–48 hours to develop. As the oils work together, the scent will change. You may even be surprised at how different it is!

Carrier Oils

Carrier oils are oils used to suspend and deliver essential oils. They are the base that you add essential oils to so they are properly diluted before being applied to your skin. Good choices for carrier oils are thin oils without a strong fragrance. Choose fractionated coconut oil, grapeseed oil, sweet almond oil, or jojoba oil to make aromatherapy perfume.

Package up a collection of four different scents in a craft paper jewelry box. Use washi tape with a message (like "With Love") to create a band on the box lid.

About the Author

Stephanie Rose is an award-winning author and the creator of Garden Therapy (*gardentherapy.ca*). Garden Therapy started as a personal blog and has bloomed into a community of craft and garden projects for people looking to add some creativity to their lives.

Originally, Stephanie started writing as a way to log her garden therapy journey while recovering from a sudden and debilitating illness. She soon connected with others who also used gardening and craft projects as therapy and shifted the blog to focus on sharing clear and helpful do-it-yourself instructions for more than 800 healthy living, gardening, and craft projects. Stephanie started making her own natural beauty products and soap in 2008 to use what was growing in the garden for personal beauty and wellness. After testing countless recipes, she has found what works best for her family and now makes all of her own soaps, lotions, scrubs, lip balms, and healing salves. Many of the natural skincare recipes she uses can be found on Garden Therapy and in the *Natural Beauty Recipe Book*, which was released in January 2016.

Stephanie lives in Vancouver, BC, where she works full-time as a writer, photographer, crafter, and artist. She can be found in her garden studio testing new recipes and creating beautiful things with natural elements. As a Master Gardener, she volunteers with a school-to-farm program that teaches inner-city children how to grow and cook their own food. At the end of the day, Stephanie enjoys every moment she can get with her family. She lives with her husband, son, and a motley crew of animals who provide her with inspiration and delight both in and out of the garden.

Library of Congress Control Number: 2018945350

We have made every effort to ensure that these instructions are accurate and complete. We cannot, however, be responsible for human error, typographical mistakes, or variations in individual work.

Production Team: Technical Editor – Katie Weeber; Graphic Artist – Ashley Millhouse; Photo Stylist – Lori Wenger; Photographer – Jason Masters.

The information in this book is not advice and should not be treated as such. Any reliance you place on such information is strictly at your own risk and not a substitute for medical, legal, or any other professional advice of any kind. What is written in this book is not intended to be substituted for the advice provided by your doctor or other health care professional. If you have any specific questions about any medical matter, you should consult your doctor or other professional healthcare provider. The author and publisher specifically disclaims all responsibility for any liability, loss, or risk, personal or otherwise, which is incurred as a consequence, directly or indirectly, of the use and application of any of this content. The views expressed in this book have not been reviewed or endorsed by the FDA or any other private or public entity.

Made in U.S.A.